ABERDEEN ART GALLERY

Guide

INTRODUCTION

*A*berdeen is a prosperous, cosmopolitan city-port in the North East of Scotland. The sea has dominated our history, through fishing, trade and the more recent development of the North Sea oil and gas industry, which has given Aberdeen its title of Oil Capital of Europe. Aberdeen is also home to innovations in technology and design and pioneering medical equipment and treatment. Despite the increasing expansion of the city, the skyline is still dominated by granite buildings, built from stone extracted from local deposits and quarries.

One of Aberdeen's most handsome granite buildings is undoubtedly the Art Gallery, designed by A. Marshall Mackenzie, and now one of the most charming Victorian galleries in the UK. When it opened in 1885, the displays combined industrial collections with art exhibitions. These were greatly enhanced by generous gifts, including Aberdeen granite merchant Alexander Macdonald's private collection of art in 1900. Macdonald was just one of several local men who made their fortune in the granite industry and associated trades and who created their own art collections based on shrewd judgement and a highly developed cultured taste. They were adventurous and daring in their collecting decisions – they bought works by contemporary artists and laid the foundations for our ongoing commitment to exhibit and collect both international and Scottish modern art.

Since its inception Aberdeen Art Gallery has benefited tremendously from the generosity of many individual benefactors along with gifts from organisations including the Contemporary Art Society. We have received grants from numerous funding bodies – such as the National Fund for Acquisitions, The Art Fund, the Scottish Arts Council and the National Collecting Scheme for Scotland – all of which have enabled us to acquire works of high calibre for the collections.

The Friends of Aberdeen Art Gallery & Museums have been magnificent supporters of the Art Gallery since the 1970s, raising funds and helping us to acquire key works, both contemporary and historic. These include William Dyce's *Lamentation Over the Dead Christ*, LS Lowry's pencil drawing of Dunottar Castle, Ian Hamilton Finlay's installation *Les Femmes de la Révolution*, an Arts and Crafts chalcedony necklace by Sybil Dunlop, the Kirkhill tea service made by George Cooper and contemporary metalwork by Michael Rowe.

As the Art Gallery celebrates its 125th anniversary, the collections it houses continue to flourish. The light and clean central space downstairs is used today to exhibit works by leading contemporary artists and the upstairs rooms hold some of the collections' earliest works.

This book provides an introduction to the wealth and diversity of these collections. As the displays change regularly and works also go out on loan, your favourite piece may not always be on exhibition, but I hope this souvenir guide will encourage you to return again and again.

Christine Rew, Art Gallery & Museums Manager

Pieter Brueghel Henry Raeburn John Everett Millais SJ Peploe Edwin Landsdeer Claude Monet

Toulouse Lautrec Damien Hirst Francis Bacon Christine Borland Fernand Léger Ben Nicholson

Where in Scotland can you see the work of all these artists under one roof?

With collections including 14th century Flemish Stations of the Cross, outstanding examples of Pre-Raphaelite art, an excellent holding of Impressionist and Post-Impressionist masterpieces, one of the finest collections of 20th century art in Britain and the most challenging contemporary art, Aberdeen Art Gallery is an exceptional centre of the visual arts in the heart of the city.

Complementing the fine art collection, the Gallery also has a collection of applied art, craft, costume and textiles. Particular strengths lie in the areas of metalwork, jewellery and enamelling, ranging from the work of early Aberdeen silversmiths to that of cutting-edge contemporary makers. An active policy of acquiring contemporary craft has resulted in one of the most stimulating collections of this type in Scotland.

David Farquharson
88

David Farquharson The Herring Fleet Leaving the Dee, Aberdeen 1888

The unique identity of Aberdeen Art Gallery, which opened in 1885, has been formed by the character of the city. For centuries, Aberdeen life revolved around the Church, its two universities (Kings College, founded in 1495 and Marischal College, founded in 1593), fishing, farming and the related industries of milling, tanning and cloth production. By the latter half of the 19th century the burgeoning granite industry was also providing income to a sizeable proportion of the community, and great wealth to a few. The men whose personal wealth was built on these various industries became the founding fathers of the city's art collections. They and their families bought works principally by contemporary, often foreign, artists and their collecting was often both adventurous and discerning.

Subsequent curators have continued this tradition of buying the best and most interesting contemporary works available to them. Their purchases have been supplemented by generous gifts and bequests, resulting in the creation of a dynamic and exciting collection of art that now spans over seven centuries.

Vecchietta Coronation of the Virgin, Annunciation & Crucifixion with Angels & Saints c.1450

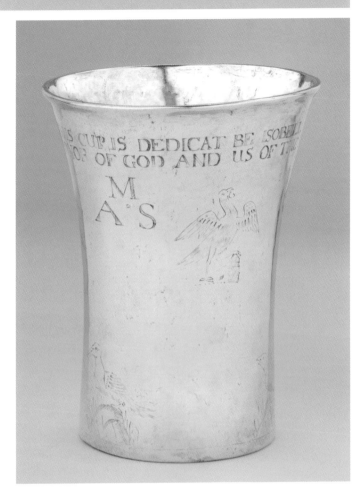

Attributed to Alexander Galloway Communion Beaker 1670-78

Today the city's economy is dominated by the oil industry, which has introduced new stimuli to Aberdeen's cultural and artistic life. In an increasingly cosmopolitan society, where a wealth of cultures coexists, Aberdeen Art Gallery is a place where art is accessible and challenging, funny and poignant, exciting and enjoyable.

William Mosman
View of Aberdeen
1756

THE EARLY COLLECTION

The collection of oil paintings dates from the 17th century to the present day. Flemish artist Pieter Brueghel the Younger is chiefly known for his copies and variants after peasant scenes by his father Pieter Brueghel the Elder and *The Faithless Shepherd* probably falls into this category. In Scotland, Aberdeen artist George Jamesone was the first figure to emerge in the 17th century as an individual artistic personality, as distinct from the craftsman-painter, and enjoyed a considerable reputation in his lifetime. In his portraits the poses and the dark settings strongly reflect Dutch painting of this period. A large view of Aberdeen by William Mosman, along with portraits by Cosmo Alexander, represent Aberdeen artists of the 18th century.

Chelsea
Hand-Painted Plate 1753-1755

Longton Hall
Quatrefoil Jug with Flowers
1754-1757

Pieter Brueghel the Younger
The Faithless Shepherd

George Robertson
Teapot c.1725

Allan Ramsay
Miss Janet Shairp 1750

Armorial Punch Bowl
1780-1791

From 1750 to the early 19th century, the collection can count works by Allan Ramsay, William Hogarth, Johann Zoffany, Sir Joshua Reynolds, Sir William Allan, Sir David Wilkie and Sir Henry Raeburn. Before the age of photography, portraiture was a particularly important genre and in the 18th century it was a means of recording wealth, status and personality. Allan Ramsay is often considered to be the premier Scottish portrait painter of the mid 18th century, a golden age of great cultural and intellectual advancements. He assimilated the delicacy of French Rococo painting into his portraits, combining this with a delightful naturalism.

Designed by J. S. Kaendler for Meissen
Figure of a Woodsman
1748-1750

William Dempster
Cake Basket 1758

Another Rococo artist, Johann Zoffany, settled in England in 1760 and made his name painting 'conversation pieces', in which a group of people are portrayed less formally than in earlier ages, engaged in conversation, playing musical instruments or reading letters. His group portrait *The Morse and Cator Family* was painted in India, although the formal trappings of the setting are conventionally British. The fine costumes and elegant interior reveal an age of gracious living.

In addition to the flowering of intellectual and artistic ideas, the 18th century witnessed a flourishing of trade, particularly the importing of Chinese tea and porcelain to Britain. European porcelain production began in the early

Johann Zoffany
The Morse and Cator Family c.1784

George Cooper
The Kirkhill Tea Service
c.1730

18th century as a direct response to demand for the very expensive Oriental product. By the middle of the century the great porcelain manufacturers of Sèvres in France and Meissen in Germany had begun to influence other European factories. Direct imitations of Meissen designs were produced by the English manufacturers Chelsea, founded in 1745 and Worcester, founded in 1751.

In 1995 the Gallery received the Cochrane Collection of 18th century European porcelain, acquired with the assistance of The Art Fund. Richmond Inglis Cochrane (1857-1936) was a passionate collector, acquiring pieces which reflected the changing styles and decorative skills of the principal European producers. His collection includes examples from the leading continental factories at Sèvres and Meissen, as well as pieces from British manufacturers such as Chelsea, Worcester and Bow.

Sir Henry Raeburn Mrs Robert Adam

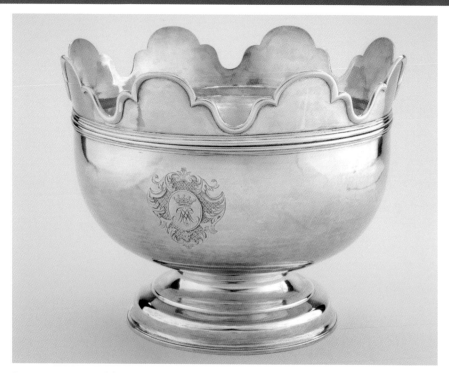

James Ker Monteith 1746-7

During the 17th and 18th centuries, tea imports increased as tea drinking became a popular social custom, initially amongst the wealthy who could afford this expensive commodity. It was fashionable to own a silver tea service, resulting in considerable business for the goldsmiths' trade (goldsmiths worked in silver as well as gold). In its quality and completeness the Kirkhill tea service, made in Aberdeen by George Cooper and said to have been acquired by the Burnett family of Kirkhill, is a unique example of Scottish provincial silver. Bullet-shaped teapots, such as that by George Robertson of Aberdeen, were especially popular in Scotland. The elegant simplicity of the design concurs with the graceful naturalism evident in the portraiture of the era.

Sir William Allan Christmas Eve

The collection also contains examples of silverwork from other parts of Scotland, particularly Edinburgh, which was the main centre for the craft. These include a rare example of a 'monteith' (a type of punchbowl with a distinctive scalloped edge), made by James Ker for the 2nd Earl of Hopetoun, and a delicately-crafted cake basket of 1758 by William Dempster. The pierced scroll-work, ornate legs and hinged handle of the cake basket highlight the exacting technical skills required of a silversmith. The 18th century collections of portraiture, landscape, porcelain and silverware reflect the tradition of patronage at this time, in which both fine art and finely crafted objects were commissioned to confirm the patron's social status and identity.

Aberdeen has an exceptional and varied collection of watercolours, spanning four centuries. The early British watercolour artists, Paul Sandby, Thomas Rowlandson, Thomas Girtin and John Robert Cozens are represented, as is the great 19th century master, J.M.W. Turner.

J.M.W. Turner
Bellinzona from the Road to Locarno 1843

David Allan
Lace workers, Rome, leaf from
A Collection of Dresses Mostly from Nature
1776

The portability of the watercolour medium lent itself well to the travelling artist and to 'on the spot' sketching; therefore many of the early watercolours were painted by artists on tour in Europe or further afield. Aberdeen Art Gallery holds a small but charming collection of portraits and landscapes relating to the British abroad on the 'The Grand Tour'.
This phenomenon, which reached its height in the 18th century, was a type of finishing school or academy for aristocratic young men. The tour involved, essentially, a trip to Paris and a circuit of the principal Italian cities: Rome, Venice, Florence and Naples.

An album of 61 watercolour drawings of traditional regional costume, created by Scottish artist David Allan when he was travelling through France and Italy between 1770 and 1776, offers a glimpse of the lighter side of The Grand Tour.

David Roberts Ancient Tartyris, Upper Egypt 1848

John Robert Cozens Villa d'Este, Tivoli 1778

The scene of Tivoli, near Rome, by John Robert Cozens alludes to the enchantment visitors to Italy experienced on catching sight of the splendid villas built by Renaissance cardinals and to the captivating landscape of that locality. Cozens combines emotional response with a mastery of technique, so that the formal dignity of his composition harmonises superbly with the painting's atmospheric quality. The poetic quality of Cozens' work stakes a claim for him as a forerunner of the Romantic Movement: his influence can be discerned in the work of J.M.W. Turner.

Of the City's four watercolours by Turner, his Romantic vision is most clearly expressed in the late watercolour of Bellinzona, the castellated town lying on the border with Italy in the Swiss canton of Ticino. Turner and the other

Romantic artists pioneered a new use of watercolour, dispensing with outline and directly exploiting the fluidity of the medium to create texture and atmosphere. Central to the composition, Bellinzona rises through vaporous mists. Glowing highlights deftly reveal where the sun catches the city walls and the Italianate towers.

David Roberts was one of the first British artists to explore the Middle East. His tour of 1838-9 resulted in numerous drawings which he used as source material for years afterwards. Roberts' approach was primarily to record the architecture: his dramatic Egyptian ruins and panoramic views possess an imaginative quality and are considered to be his finest works. *Ancient Tartyris, Upper Egypt* is a good example of his Egyptian subjects and illustrates the way in which he exaggerated the already awe-inspiring dimensions of the ancient sites to present them on a superhuman scale. Aberdeen also holds significant figure studies in watercolour by Sir David Wilkie, who travelled to the Orient in 1840, and beautiful sketches of ancient Moorish architecture and local inhabitants produced by Scots artist William Allan, who in 1834 realised his ambition to visit Spain.

James Giles 1801 - 1870

James Giles was the highly talented son of a designer at the local calico-printing factory in Woodside, Aberdeen. During his lifetime, Giles was one of the most prominent of the Aberdeen artists – his patrons included landed aristocracy and Queen Victoria – but he has been little remembered in subsequent surveys of Scottish art. This is due in part to the fact that he spent most of his working life in Aberdeen, unlike his contemporaries who left the North East to find fame in London.

Aberdeen Art Gallery holds the largest collection of the artist's work in existence (almost 300 works), including numerous sketches and watercolours as well as portraits and landscapes in oil. A versatile artist, Giles was also a successful landscape architect, designing a number of gardens for estates in Aberdeenshire and monuments in the city of Aberdeen.

However, Giles' spiritual home was Italy where he spent three years from 1823 to 1826. The bright, Italian light fascinated him and all of the sketches and watercolours that resulted from his sojourn are enlivened by a free and sensitive treatment that captures the distinctive Mediterranean atmosphere.

James Giles
In the Forum, Rome 1824

VICTORIAN ART

*T*he Victorians are famed for the variety of their taste in art. This is borne out by the artists of the period, whose work covers all aspects of life, fantasy and fiction. Queen Victoria's interests, in common with the wider Victorian public, lay in sentimental and narrative art. Aberdeen Art Gallery has one of the best collections of Victorian narrative art, with particularly good examples of the contemporary crazes for Orientalism and for all things Scottish.

Sir Edwin Landseer
Flood in the Highlands

Sir David Wilkie
The Turkish Letter Writer
1840

Fascination for the exoticism of the Near East continued throughout the 19th century, creating a discipline of Orientalist painting. *The Turkish Letter Writer*, by Sir David Wilkie, is a case in point. The influence of the East can also be seen in artefacts of the period: the 19th century silver collection demonstrates how goods imported from the East shaped the type of objects produced, such as William Jamieson's spice box with integral nutmeg grater. Jamieson was a prolific goldsmith in Aberdeen from 1806-41 and also a successful businessman, setting up the firm which still trades today as Jamieson & Carry in the city's Union Street.

Joseph Farquharson
The Hour of Prayer – Interior of the Mosque of Sultan Beni Hassan, Cairo 1888

Dress c.1840

William Jamieson
Spice Box c.1810

Joseph Farquharson's reputation as a painter is based on his masterful snowscapes which earned him the nickname 'Frozen Mutton'. Aberdeen holds a number of landscapes by Farquharson, many of which depict the Forest of Birse on the Finzean estate, near Aberdeen. However, even well into the late Victorian period, the lure of the East still attracted artists and one of the most impressive Victorian paintings at Aberdeen is Farquharson's large, ambitious canvas *The Hour of Prayer*.

John Phillip Baptism in Scotland 1850

David Wilkie pioneered 'genre' painting: subjects from everyday life, depicted with a homely simplicity and sharp observation of character. This type of storytelling or narrative picture was to become highly popular in the Victorian era and reflected the taste of that time for paintings rich in colour, action and drama. Aberdeen-born John 'Spanish' Phillip began his career painting in the manner of Wilkie. Aberdeen Art Gallery has a large collection of Phillip's work, including his early Scottish pieces, such as the genre painting with political overtones, *Baptism in Scotland* and his later Spanish paintings, which marked a revolution in his style. In the former, Phillip has depicted a Presbyterian family baptism taking place in a Highland home. Religion played a large part in Victorian life. The Disruption of 1843, when a schism in the Church of Scotland resulted in the creation of the Free Church, saw the production of

John Phillip La Bomba 1863

works commemorating the conflict and its effects. These include Middleton Rettie's Disruption brooch and a brass baptismal bowl from St Clements Church in Aberdeen, which was the first Free Church to be built in Scotland after the Disruption.

In Phillip's later, Spanish paintings, much more emphasis is placed on rich colour, vivacity, painterly technique and sumptuous costume. *La Bomba* shows the influence of the Spanish 17th century master Diego Velasquez in the confident handling of the girl's striped silk dress and the man's thickly

Brass Baptismal Bowl
c.1843

M. Rettie & Sons
Disruption Brooch 1845

James Erskine
Snuff Box c.1810

encrusted epaulettes, embroidered in gold and silver thread. The Victorians appreciated fine fabrics and fashions and in this industrial age of mass production, fashionable clothes became more widely available. The City's collection of costume follows the development of 19th century fashion, with its distinctive features of crinoline and bustle dresses accompanied by shawls and accessories.

The Victorians liked to commemorate events of note and many items commissioned as mementoes have found their way into the collections. Often, inscriptions on these pieces tell us why they were highly prized. A gold snuff box made by James Erskine, for example, was presented to William Knight by his students in 1811, as a token of support after he failed to be appointed Professor of Natural History at Marischal College, Aberdeen.

William McTaggart A Ground Swell, Carradale 1883-86

Highlights of Aberdeen Art Gallery's holding of Victorian narrative painting include the monumental *Flood in the Highlands* by Sir Edwin Landseer, one of the most popular of romantic painters, who specialised in animal painting and scenes of the Scottish Highlands. The Victorian collection is also rich in examples of paintings by the Edinburgh School, Robert Scott Lauder and his pupils. Lauder became Master of the Trustees Academy in Edinburgh in 1852 and was soon displaying the kind of talent and charisma that had a magnetic effect on brilliant students. The principal members of this group were William Quiller Orchardson, John Pettie, William McTaggart, George Paul Chalmers and Hugh Cameron. For the Victorian English public, the works of those gifted young artists established the concept of a 'Scotch' School - a dexterous style, clever in handling, exploiting sketchy draughtsmanship and pure, rather than diluted, colours.

THE PRE-RAPHAELITES & their followers

*I*n 1848 a small group of English artists came together and set out to recapture the beauty and simplicity of the medieval world. They wanted to combine the pious qualities of medieval art with their own study of nature and the world around them. What they created was a body of art that was full of literary symbolism, bright colours and minute detail – paintings that today are immediately recognisable and greatly loved.

D.G. Rossetti
Mariana 1870

John William Waterhouse Penelope and her Suitors 1912

The Pre-Raphaelites represented at Aberdeen Art Gallery include the principal members of the Brotherhood – Dante Gabriel Rossetti, William Holman Hunt and John Everett Millais – as well as other artists who were associated with the movement, most notably William Dyce and John William Waterhouse.

The Pre-Raphaelite movement underwent several phases, varying between precise, almost photographic, minutely detailed paintings, such as *Titian's First Essay in Colouring* by William Dyce and more austere images in the manner of the early Italian masters. *Mariana* by D.G. Rossetti exemplifies the late medievalising strand of 'Aesthetic Pre-Raphaelitism', which in turn produced the Arts & Crafts movement. Rossetti emphasised themes of sensuous medievalism and techniques that created a dream-like atmosphere.

William Dyce
Titian's First Essay in Colouring 1856-57

Ann Macbeth
Silver and Amethyst Necklace
1905

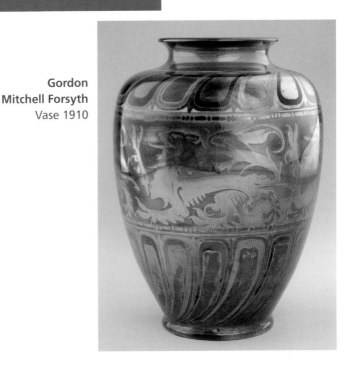

**Gordon
Mitchell Forsyth**
Vase 1910

Rossetti's model for this picture, and his real life muse, was Janey Morris, an Arts & Crafts embroiderer who was the wife of his friend and fellow artist William Morris. Rossetti's romantic attachment to Janey was particularly strong around the time that this work was painted in 1870 and her unusual beauty continued to obsess him.

The Arts and Crafts Movement, which had been established by William Morris, Rossetti and Burne-Jones, continued to espouse their ideals of truth to nature and material into the 20th century. An array of intricate jewellery and enamelling by the Aberdeen artist James Cromar Watt reflects the fine precision of Arts and Crafts artists. This was a movement in which, for the first time, women makers excelled and many turned their hand to a variety of disciplines: metalwork, jewellery, enamelling, embroidery and bookbinding. The city's collection contains examples of work by

Liberty
Athelstan Wardrobe c.1902

Phoebe Anna Traquair
Sanctuary pendant 1902

Ann Macbeth, Sybil Dunlop, Ernestine Mills and Jessie M. King. The gem-like enamel pendant above shows the skill and vision of the leading female Arts and Crafts exponent in Scotland, Phoebe Anna Traquair.

Aberdeen Art Gallery also holds Arts and Crafts furniture which, in contrast to the jewellery of the period, is functional as well as decorative. This is apparent in the honest simplicity of a Liberty wardrobe, the natural unpolished oak of which is echoed in an ornamental, hand-stained upper panel depicting a wooded landscape. The distinctive, brightly coloured, hand-painted pots produced at the pottery studios, Mak'Merry and Bough in the Lothians, are typical examples of Arts and Crafts ceramics. This collection is further augmented by lustre ware from Pilkington's Lancastrian Tile and Pottery Works.

William Dyce 1806 - 1864

William Dyce is often considered to be the forefather of the Pre-Raphaelites and it was he who persuaded the influential art critic, John Ruskin, of the merits of Pre-Raphaelite art in 1855.

Born in Aberdeen in 1806, the son of a medical professor, Dyce studied medicine and theology at Marischal College in Aberdeen. After a brief period of study in London he went to Rome, where he was influenced by a group of German painters, the Nazarenes. Like them, Dyce wanted to promote a style of art that had the purity and spiritual intensity of the early Italian masters of the 15th century.

William Dyce
Beatrice 1859

Aberdeen Art Gallery has the largest collection of Dyce's work in the world, encompassing portraits, paintings of medieval, religious, mythological and historical subject matter, landscapes and studies for his ambitious frescoes for the House of Lords, the Palace of Westminster, All Saints' Church on Margaret Street, London and Osborne House.

James Cromar Watt 1862 - 1940

James Cromar Watt was an architect, designer, jeweller and enameller who dedicated his life to the promotion of the arts in the North East of Scotland. Watt initially trained as an architect after leaving Aberdeen Grammar School in 1878. Following a series of trips to Italy he returned to Britain and was admitted to the Architectural School of the Royal Academy in London. Watt then embarked on a tour of Greece where he became increasingly interested in ornamentation - his designs and sketches focused less on architecture, as he began to concentrate on becoming skilled in several craft disciplines.

James Cromar Watt
Turquoise and Enamel
Necklace c.1905-9

The vast collection of enamel work and jewellery by Watt at Aberdeen Art Gallery demonstrates his superb craftsmanship. A fascination with animal imagery – such as serpents, peacocks and dragons – was incorporated into the stylised Arts & Crafts method in his enamelled plaques, pendants and bracelets. Combining gold with jewel-like enamel and precious and semi-precious stones, Watt produced sumptuous jewellery in both subtle and strident colours. His use of symmetry and fine materials resulted in timeless works of art. In 1941 Aberdeen Art Gallery received the James Cromar Watt Bequest, a group of decorative art objects that Watt collected whilst travelling through Europe and Asia. Highlights include Chinese lacquer ware and Venetian glass.

Oriental Lacquer Box
18th century

PEASANTS & PRIVILEGE

*A*berdeen Art Gallery houses one of the foremost collections of Realist art in the country. This is because our earliest patrons collected innovative, contemporary painting of the time and also because Scottish artists studied in France and in the Netherlands; in this way, Scottish art assimilated the new movement.

Henri H. La Thangue
The Plough Boy c.1900

Jules Bastien-Lepage Going to School 1882

From the revolutions that spread through Europe in 1848 came new attitudes to class structure, politics, morals and fashion. It was an age in which barriers were broken; a restless age of dissatisfaction and discontent. Shifts in political thought, and especially the rise of Socialism, were clearly reflected in artistic movements. As in Henri la Thangue's *The Ploughboy*, studies of ordinary people, grand in scale but in everyday settings, raised the status of the working man or woman; their epic depiction suggested heroism and innate nobility.

Of all the French Realist artists, Jules Bastien-Lepage was the one who most influenced his British counterparts and this was particularly true of his Scottish disciples, John Lavery and James Guthrie. His paintings, which are distinguished by a solitary figure, high viewpoint, large scale and use of square brushes, find their echo in numerous paintings of the Scottish and English Realist schools.

Guthrie's acknowledged masterpiece, *To Pastures New*, owes much to the Realist painters of the Low Countries. His novel approach lay in combining the flat landscapes and uniform colours of Dutch art with figures seen very close up and on a large scale, as French artists, such as Bastien-Lepage, preferred. In spite of the modest subject matter, the ponderous birds and their herd-girl have, through the artist's handling of them, achieved the monumentality of a processional frieze.

Sir John Lavery The Tennis Party 1885

Yet Realist art was not always trying to show the heroism of the poor or to moralise. Sometimes it was attempting to do something even more modern – just to capture a moment in time, a real scene at a particular time of day. In this way Realism can come very close to Impressionism.

Lavery's now famous painting, *The Tennis Party,* certainly exhibits one lesson that he had learned from his French hero Bastien-Lepage: to capture movement and a moment in time. Rather than the noble peasant, Lavery chose the leisured classes as his subject, but in spite of this, his overriding concern to convey a seemingly spontaneous moment of real life makes this now iconic painting a quintessential example of Realist art.

Sir James Guthrie To Pastures New 1883

John Singer Sargent Mrs J.W. Crombie 1898

Robert Brough
A Sulky Girl c.1896

The artistic style and modern ideas of these movements also spilled over into portraiture. Although the turn of the century and the Edwardian era witnessed the beginnings of the decline of the aristocracy, the portrait was still central to their status. John Singer Sargent developed the flamboyant 'swagger portrait', with virtuoso sweeping brushwork, dramatic lighting and spontaneous poses. His friend, the Aberdeen painter Robert Brough, who shared Sargent's bold style and admiration for the Spanish 17th century master Velasquez, painted portraits of the wealthiest members of Aberdeen society.

FRENCH IMPRESSIONISM & POST-IMPRESSIONISM

Pierre Auguste Renoir
La Roche Guyon 1885-1886

*P*ossibly one of the best known of artistic movements, Impressionism emerged in Paris during the second half of the 19th century. As young men, the Impressionist artists were experimenting with new methods of painting, seeking visual truth in colour and light. This apparently simple desire - to paint what they could actually see - was a dramatic break away from the then popular subjects of imagined narrative and historical scenes.

Claude Monet
La Falaise à Fécamp 1881

The Impressionists admired the landscapes of Corot, Boudin and the other artists of the French Realist Barbizon school, who concentrated on painting ordinary working people in everyday settings. However, contemporary critics found the Impressionists' studies of ordinary people and modern life sketchy and unfinished. Today of course they are the most highly prized art works in the world and are traded internationally, their images almost too familiar. Thus Van Gogh's sunflowers and Monet's water lilies may have lost some of

Alfred Sisley Une Cour aux Sablons 1885

their magic, but coming across a less familiar work by the same artist can stun the viewer anew. These pictures still have the freshness and allure that they had when first painted and seeing a collection of them, as is possible at Aberdeen Art Gallery, continues to be for most lovers of art an intensely enjoyable and stimulating experience.

From around 1870, Monet, Renoir and Sisley all began the practice of painting *en plein air* – with Monet sometimes working on several canvases simultaneously – producing not so much a series of landscape views as a record of the effects of weather and daylight. *La Falaise à Fécamp* is

Henri Marie Raymond de Toulouse-Lautrec
Charles Conder - Sketch for 'Aux Ambassadeurs: Gens Chic' 1893

Auguste Rodin
L'Homme qui Marche 1877

one in a series of cliff paintings showing Monet's masterful rendition of changing atmospheric conditions. In the 1880s, Renoir began to look to new developments in Post-Impressionist circles, employing the distinctive rainbow palette and 'broken colour': small strokes of different tints that merge at a distance.

Marie Laurencin
La Guitare 1936

An extremely fine and rare example of Renoir's landscape painting, *La Roche Guyon*, illustrates very effectively his use of pure colour and a vibrant palette at this critical time in his career.

By the end of the 19th century, the Impressionists had become figures with worldwide reputations and the frontiers of avant-garde art were constantly being extended. A certain mannerism entered their work, with exaggerated use of colour and line. Rhythmic movement was created by the use of parallel strokes of paint. Perspective was flattened and broad areas of single colour replaced the earlier practice of broken colour technique. Thus Impressionism led to Post-Impressionism.

Fernand Léger Nature Morte avec Vase 1925

Pierre Bonnard Vernonnet – Paysage près de Giverny 1924

Some artists, such as Pierre Bonnard and Eduard Vuillard (dubbed *intimistes*, due to the private, intimate nature of their paintings), continued in a Post-Impressionistic style, but surpassed Impressionism in their vibrant use of colour. Others, such as Fernand Léger, embraced the flat, ambiguous and three-dimensional forms of Cubism. This radical movement, that was ultimately to lead to complete abstraction, was invented by Pablo Picasso and Georges Braque in Paris at the start of the 20th century. Modern Art had arrived.

The Scottish Colourists

George Leslie Hunter
Still Life – Roses and a Black Fan

John Duncan Fergusson
In the Sunlight 1907

The four Scottish artists **S.J. Peploe, J.D. Fergusson, G.L. Hunter and F.C.B Cadell** have achieved tremendous critical acclaim over the last few decades. Their art is bright, colourful and easily accessible. Groundbreaking exhibitions have popularised it, both in Scotland and further afield. Despite the diversity of their styles and their relatively independent careers, the Colourists form an identifiable movement, which was to have an enormous effect on 20th century Scottish artists including John Maclaughlin Milne, William Gillies, John Maxwell and Anne Redpath. The Colourists' distinctive landscape and still life paintings employed thick paint, strong colour and bold brushwork. Their influence is still apparent in Scottish painting today, with several professional artists continuing in the same tradition.

At Aberdeen Art Gallery there is a strong collection of work by the Scottish Colourists and in particular the work of S.J. Peploe; all phases of his career are represented, from early, dark-toned portraits inspired by Whistler, to several Iona seascapes, landscapes and timeless flower studies.

Samuel John Peploe Landscape Cassis c.1924

EARLY 20th CENTURY

The 20th century saw the arrival of Modernism in art and a host of new, progressive movements and styles in step with the radical social and political changes of the era. Aberdeen Art Gallery holds a wide-ranging assembly of British Modern art – with some of the best examples in the country of works by Paul Nash, Ben Nicholson, Stanley Spencer and Francis Bacon, in addition to the Scottish Colourists, Joan Eardley and the Edinburgh School of the 1960s.

Gwendoline John
Seated Girl Holding
a Piece of Sewing
1915-25

Robert Polhill Bevan
Ploughing on the Downs c.1907

A group of artists working in London in the 1910s, known as the Camden Town Group - Spencer Frederick Gore, Robert Polhill Bevan and Walter Richard Sickert amongst them - absorbed the influences of the French Impressionists and Post-Impressionists and incorporated their artistic styles when painting English scenes. These painters focused on aspects of modern life: modern male-female relationships, gritty urban life and the transitional mood of London around the time of World War I.

Augustus John was briefly associated with the Camden Town Group, but along with fellow artists James Dickson Innes and Derwent Lees, formed a

Augustus John The Blue Pool 1911

triumvirate dedicated to a new English Romanticism. They shared subject matter, travelled together in Wales and Europe and developed a deliberately naïve, primitive aesthetic. John was held to be an artistic genius in the 1920s and *The Blue Pool* shows the artist at the height of his powers, but within a few years his work was surpassed by his more progressive contemporaries, such as Paul Nash. Nash studied art at the Slade School in London amongst a distinguished class of students that included Stanley Spencer and Edward Wadsworth. During the 1930s he and his circle established an avant-garde movement in British art. Under the influence of Cubism and Surrealism, Nash developed a deeply personal vision of the natural world. His *Wood on the Downs*, at Aberdeen Art Gallery, is considered an iconic painting.

Paul Nash
Wood on
the Downs 1929

Sir Stanley Spencer Southwold 1937

James McBey 1883-1959

James McBey Venetian Night 1930

James McBey was inspired to sketch, paint and etch by his numerous sojourns abroad. A largely self-taught artist, McBey was born in Newburgh, to the north of Aberdeen, in 1883. His youth was one of hardship and emotional deprivation. He was the illegitimate son of a young woman, Annie Gillespie, who was blind and suffered from severe depression – she eventually hanged herself. Although her suicide was a great shock, it released McBey from his responsibility to her and he seized the opportunity to escape the drudgery of a job in banking and set off to find his fortune. This he did through travelling abroad and depicting the places and people he encountered in etchings, watercolours and oil paintings. After a long, varied and successful career McBey died at his home in Tangiers in 1959. His wife Marguerite (née Loeb), also an artist, funded the construction and furnishing of Aberdeen Art Gallery's McBey Print Room and Library in his memory. She also gifted much of her husband's work to the Gallery. Over the next forty years she donated further items and a substantial sum of money for the purpose of enhancing the City's art collections and the cultural and artistic experiences of Gallery visitors. A selection of McBey's paintings is on permanent display in the Print Room and occasional changing displays highlight various aspects of his prodigious output.

James Cowie Two Schoolgirls 1934-35

The devastation of the Second World War found expression in the ever-darkening and intensely personal work of war-time artists. The paintings of this period in the collection by James Cowie, Paul Nash, John Minton, L.S. Lowry and Eric Ravilious – Nash's pupil, who sought to capture a nostalgic vision of England - have in common a sombre, austere colour palette and varying degrees of Surrealist or Romantic tendencies.

Sir William Gillies
Dusk c.1959

Anne Redpath
White Cyclamen 1962

Francis Bacon Pope I – Study after Pope Innocent X by Velasquez 1951

Joan Eardley and Catterline

Scottish artist **Joan Eardley's** celebrated images of Glasgow children form one half of her output, the other being the dynamic seascapes painted in the Kincardineshire village of Catterline. These two contrasting aspects of her work are represented in the Art Gallery collections.

Eardley visited Catterline in 1950 and soon afterwards established a studio there. Other painters followed in her wake and for a fleeting moment this small fishing village had the status of an artists' colony. Excited by wild seas and weather, Eardley painted her elemental seascapes in the open air, in front of her subject. Her work became increasingly expressionistic but never lost that sense of place which came from acute observation. She worked continuously, painting and drawing in all weathers. A generous gift of a selection of her drawings and on-the-spot studies was given to Aberdeen Art Gallery by the artist's sister. They are working drawings and were not intended for exhibition, but they allow a valuable insight into Eardley's artistic practice and enhance our experience of her work.

Joan Eardley
High Tide,
A Winter Afternoon 1961

Ben Nicholson Still Life on Table 1947

Abstraction became a new force in Post-War art. Ben Nicholson's *March 14 – 47 (Still Life on Table)* and sculptures in the collection by Barbara Hepworth, including *Oval Form, Trezion* (dramatically displayed in a marble fountain which Hepworth designed especially for Aberdeen Art Gallery's Centre Court), show how artists began to interpret subjects in a pared-down, simplified manner, one in which form and feeling became the most vital.

Eric Ravilious Train Landscape 1940

Dame Barbara Hepworth
Oval Form – Trezion 1962

Aberdeen Art Gallery Guide

Frank Auerbach
J.Y.M. Seated 1976

he exciting developments in late 20th century art and crafts reflect the humour, passion, wars, poetry, humanity and social freedoms of the Post-Modern age. Frank Auerbach's dynamic, raw portrait *J.Y.M. Seated* exemplifies the Expressionist style that swept through the 1960s and 70s. The refugee German Jewish artist painted Juliet Yardley Mills, known as J.Y.M. to her friends, every week over a period from 1963.

Peter Howson
Serb and Muslim 1994

In the last two decades of the 20th century, Scottish artists continued
the painterly tradition, although styles evolved rapidly in new directions:
Peter Howson's *Serb & Muslim* exploits all the power and expressiveness
of paint on canvas to capture a brutal, crushing image from the Croatian
War, while Alison Watt's *Rivière*, a quiet contemplation of drapery,
merely hints at the female body: the resulting impression is subtle yet
intensely erotic.

LATER MODERN ART

Although installation art had first appeared in the 'ready made' or 'found' objects of Marcel Duchamp in the early 20th century, towards the end of the century, the installation became a more and more popular art form. Christine Borland's *Five Set Conversation Pieces* – five foetal skulls and pelvises crafted in bone china – was inspired by a visit the artist made to Liverpool Museum, where she saw examples of delicately painted china bowls commemorating ships' maiden voyages. The pieces refer to the trading of goods, including slaves, but also draw on Borland's own personal experience: at the time she created this work she had recently given birth to her first child. In this way, the artist makes a humanist statement as well as a personal one.

As late 20th century artists searched for new media to express their ideas, boundaries between fine art and craft became increasingly blurred and the (sometimes ironic) references to traditional artistic movements became woven into the language of Post Modern art.

Christine Borland Five Set Conversation Pieces 1998

Alison Watt Rivière 2000

Malcolm Appleby
Gold Feather Necklace 1980

William Littlejohn
Fish Lantern Sunset 1987

Aberdeen Art Gallery's collecting of contemporary craft began in earnest in the 1980s with a particular focus on metalwork and jewellery. The highly regarded collection embraces innovative work by young jewellers and metalworkers, as well as that by influential and established makers.

The Gallery has acquired a body of work by one of the country's leading craftsmen, Malcolm Appleby. Much of Appleby's output is inspired by nature and for many years he lived locally at Crathes on Deeside, an area famed for its natural beauty. An engraver and designer in precious metals, he creates intricate and often amusing objects with flair and great skill. His engraving techniques were honed when he was apprenticed as a gun engraver and may be seen to stunning effect in his gold feather necklace. Like many designer-silversmiths, he often collaborates with other makers and designers, in this case Peter Doyle.

Archie Brennan
Aberdeen 1964

Wendy Ramshaw
Chain of Glass Tears
for Weeping Woman 1998

The innovative approach of Wendy Ramshaw, a leading artist-jeweller, has had an appreciable influence on modern jewellery. In 1988 she began a ten year project which resulted in the creation of a series of works termed *Picasso's Ladies*, based on the artist's paintings of his principal muses. The striking necklace, *Chain of Glass Tears for Weeping Woman*, is Ramshaw's reaction to *Weeping Woman* (1937), a portrait of Dora Maar. The inspiration for its tear shape came from a glass droplet which was once part of a Victorian chandelier.

The City's collection of late 20th century tapestries includes many that were woven at the renowned Dovecot Studios in Edinburgh. Archie Brennan had just become Director of the Dovecot when he was commissioned by Aberdeen Town Council to design and weave a tapestry for the Art Gallery. Thus, *Aberdeen 1964* is an important piece in the history of modern tapestry weaving. This tapestry, his first major commission, endeavours to portray the essence of Aberdeen, capturing movement in the falling leaves set against grey granite and blue sea.

Bill Gibb 1943 - 1988

Brought up on a farm near New Pitsligo in Aberdeenshire, **Bill Gibb** showed a precocious talent for art and design and set off for London at the age of nineteen to attend St Martin's School of Art. He was to become one of the foremost fashion designers of his generation, clothing celebrities such as Twiggy, Bianca Jagger and Elizabeth Taylor with his romantic layers of multi-patterned fabrics. He never forgot his Scottish roots and the influence of traditionally Scottish fabrics – such as tweed and tartan – may be seen in his renowned collection of 1970, which gained him the title 'Designer of the Year', and in his Scottish Collection of 1978.

The Art Gallery holds the largest collection of his garments along with a major portfolio of his drawings, including sketches and finished designs. These show how his ideas evolved and demonstrate his careful attention to detail. As he explained in an interview for Vogue Magazine in 1976: "A collection is three months of solid graft. Picking the fabrics, making roughly 200 sketches and boiling them down to 50 or 60, then turning them into reality."

Bill Gibb
Gypsy Dress
1969

In the early 1980s, Gibb's popularity declined as he battled ill-health and his layered outfits fell from favour. His untimely death at the age of 44 robbed the fashion world of a creative genius.

Jim Lambie Head & Shoulders (with Conditioner) 2003

Turner Prize winners and nominees Tracey Emin, Damien Hirst, Nathan Coley and the Chapman Brothers are just a selection of the major contemporary British artists whose audacious art works contrast so effectively with the classical columns of the Art Gallery's Centre Court.

Fun and light hearted, serious or sensitive – pieces by established and emerging British artists such as Julian Opie, Gavin Turk, Jim Lambie and Dalziel & Scullion captivate and move visitors to the Gallery. Jim Lambie's *Head & Shoulders (with Conditioner)*, an installation of old LP sleeves with blacked-

Torsten Lauschmann Pandora's Ball 2008

out text, has proved to be a popular puzzle-piece for nostalgia lovers; the extraordinary realism of Gavin Turk's bronze sleeping bag *Habitat* is a thought-provoking observation on the 'haves and have nots' of our society.

The Gallery has an ambitious and dynamic contemporary applied art collection which encompasses metalwork, jewellery, glass, ceramics and textiles. Representing a large number of UK and international makers, the collection is especially strong in its selection of metalwork and jewellery. Over

Julian Opie
Sara Walking 2003

the last decade collecting has focused on makers who ma
combine tradition with a modern approach, harnessing n
to work their material in exciting and innovative ways. Th
collection has been enlarged through a series of purchase
commissions, some of which are direct responses to the
whilst others commemorate anniversaries and special eve
Stewart's *Bird Bowl*, which celebrates the 25th Annivers
Aberdeen Art Gallery & Museums.

Vladimir Bohm
Fine Silver and Vitreous
Enamel Vessel 2003

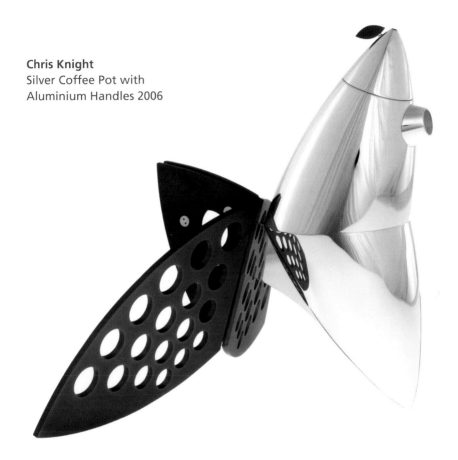

Chris Knight
Silver Coffee Pot with
Aluminium Handles 2006

British metalworkers, including Graham Stewart, Pamela Rawnsley and Chris Knight, are represented alongside European makers Vladimir Bohm, Simone ten Hompel and David Huycke. The collection contains items illustrating international developments in contemporary metalwork, with pieces by Junko Mori, Toru Kaneko, Hiroshi Suzuki, Robert Foster, Marian Hosking and William Lee who represent Japan, Australia and Korea. Fascinated with nature and their immediate environment, these makers often wish to communicate an environmental, cultural or political message through their objects.

Hiroshi Suzuki Aqua Poesy VI 2004

Graham Stewart
Commemorative Bird Bowl 2000-2001

**Jacqueline
Ryan**
Neckpiece
2008

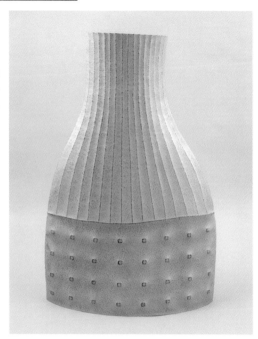

Toru Kaneko
Tall Tin-plated Copper Vase
2004

Work by renowned jewellers Dorothy Hogg, Peter Chang and David Watkins and rising artist Jacqueline Ryan showcase the achievement of British jewellers, whilst Nora Fok and Yoko Izawa push the boundaries of traditional jewellery by utilising non-precious materials, such as lycra and acrylic, in their work.

In addition to metalwork and jewellery the collection holds significant examples of contemporary glass and ceramics by makers including Keiko Mukaide, Takahiro Kondo, Stephen Bird, Kate Malone and Ken Eastman.

Aberdeen Art Gallery's collections policy of acquiring work, not only from Britain but also from abroad, enables the Gallery to present both fine and applied art in an international context. This gives visitors the opportunity to view new and exciting works, from both established and up-and-coming artists and makers.

Page 1 Lucie Rie *Stoneware Bottle Vase c.1980* National Fund for Acquisitions © The Estate of Lucie Rie.

Pages 8 & 9 David Farquharson *Herring Fleet Leaving the Dee, Aberdeen 1888* National Fund for Acquisitions, The Art Fund: Ramsay-Dyce Bequest.

Page 11 Attributed to Alexander Galloway *Communion Beaker 1670-78* Friends of Aberdeen Art Gallery & Museums, National Fund for Acquisitions, The Art Fund.

Page 14 Longton Hall *Quatrefoil Jug with Flowers 1754-1757* The Art Fund. Chelsea *Hand-Painted Plate 1753-1755.* The Art Fund.

Page 15 George Robertson *Teapot c.1725* The Art Fund.

Page 17 *Armorial Punch Bowl 1780-1791* The Art Fund.

Page 18 Designed by J S. Kaendler for Meissen *Figure of a Woodsman 1748-1750.* The Art Fund. **William Dempster** *Cake Basket 1758.* National Fund for Acquisitions, The Art Fund.

Page 20 George Cooper *The Kirkhill Tea Service c.1730* Incorporation of Goldsmiths of the City of Edinburgh, Friends of Aberdeen Art Gallery & Museums, The Art Fund.

Page 21 Sir Henry Raeburn *Mrs Robert Adam* National Fund for Acquisitions, The Art Fund: Ramsay-Dyce Bequest.

Page 24 J.M.W. Turner *Bellinzona from the Road to Locarno 1843* The Art Fund.

Page 25 David Allan *Lace workers, Rome, leaf from A Collection of Dresses Mostly from Nature 1776*
National Fund for Acquisitions, The Art Fund.

Page 33 William Jamieson *Spice Box c.1810* National Fund for Acquisitions.

Page 36 M. Rettie & Sons *Disruption Brooch 1845* National Fund for Acquisitions. **James Erskine,** *Snuff Box c.1810* Friends of Aberdeen Art Gallery & Museums.

Page 41 Ann Macbeth *Silver and Amethyst Necklace 1905* Friends of Aberdeen Art Gallery & Museums, National Fund for Acquisitions. **Gordon Mitchell Forsyth** *Vase 1910* National Fund for Acquisitions.

Page 42 Liberty *Athelstan Wardrobe c.1902* National Fund for Acquisitions. **Phoebe Anna Traquair** *Sanctuary* pendant *1902* National Fund for Acquisitions.

Page 44 James Cromar Watt *Turquoise and Enamel Necklace c.1905-9* The Art Fund, National Fund for Acquisitions.

Page 45 William Brodie Ruth (detail) 1872.

Page 49 Sir John Lavery *The Tennis Party 1885.* By courtesy of Felix Rosenstiel's Widow & Son Ltd, London on behalf of the Estate of Sir John Lavery.

Page 55 Claude Monet *La Falaise à Fécamp 1881* Museums and Art Galleries Commission.

Page 58 Marie Laurencin *La Guitare 1936* © ADAGP, Paris and DACS, London 2009.

Page 59 Fernand Léger *Nature Morte avec Vase 1925* © ADAGP, Paris and DACS, London 2009.

Page 60 Pierre Bonnard *Vernonnet – Paysage près de Giverny 1924* National Fund for Acquisitions, The Art Fund: Ramsay-Dyce Bequest © ADAGP, Paris and DACS, London 2009.

Page 61 Emile-Antoine Bourdelle *Herakles drawing his bow against the Stymphalian Birds* (detail) 1908 - 1909.

Page 62 John Duncan Fergusson *In the Sunlight 1907* © The Fergusson Gallery, Perth & Kinross Council.

Page 66 Augustus Edwin John *The Blue Pool 1911* © The estate of Augustus John, Bridgeman Art.

Page 67 Paul Nash *Wood on the Downs 1929* © Tate, London 2009. **Sir Stanley Spencer** *Southwold 1937* © The Estate of Stanley Spencer 2009. All rights reserved DACS.

Page 68 James McBey *Venetian Night 1930* © Family of James and Marguerite McBey.

Page 69 James Cowie *Two Schoolgirls 1934-35* © The Artist's Estate.

Page 70 Sir William Gillies *Dusk c.1959* © Royal Scottish Academy. **Anne Redpath** *White Cyclamen 1962* © Royal Scottish Academy and Bridgeman Art Gallery.

Page 71 Francis Bacon *Pope I – Study after Pope Innocent X by Velasquez 1951* Contemporary Art Society © The Estate of Francis Bacon. All rights reserved. DACS 2009.

Page 72 Joan Eardley *High Tide, A Winter Afternoon 1961* © The Eardley Estate.